An Apple a Day

an apple

mela
manzana
pomme

25 Surprisingly Universal
Idioms & Their Origins

a day

Written and translated by
MICHELA TARTAGLIA

Illustrations by
DANIELE SIMONELLI

SASQUATCH BOOKS | SEATTLE

To my nonna Rosa, who fed us with bread and idioms religiously never explained, and to my sister, Rossella, the true linguist in our family.

CONTENTS

44 → 49

Talk of an angel and you'll hear the fluttering of its wings

50 → 53

As you sow, so shall you reap

54 → 57

The pitcher will go to the well once too often

58 → 61

Appetite comes with eating

62 → 67

To split hairs

68 → 71

The grass is always greener
on the other side

72 → 77

Don't poke the bear

78 → 81

If you lie down with dogs,
you'll get up with fleas

82 → 85

When the cat's away,
the mice will play

86 → 89

Kill two birds with one stone

90 → 95

Bats in the belfry

96 → 99

Don't look a gift horse
in the mouth

100 → 105

Don't cast your pearls
before swine

106 → 111

When in Rome,
do as the Romans do

112 → 115

A leopard can't
change its spots

INTRODUCTION

Donna Baffuta Sempre Piaciuta / *A Woman with a Mustache Always Has Prospects*

⟶

WHY DO WE SAY THAT?

It's a popular Italian sentiment that hairy or bearded women are attractive and fascinating. The Italian expression, which is not without humor and irony, stresses how natural beauty wins out against modern beauty and makeup techniques. Whether the woman is a femme fatale or a "dark lady," hairy or not, she will always be the inspiring muse of countless artistic creations.

The art of translation happens when one is driven by a love of words: they can be flowing and recondite, sweet and sour, ancient and neologistic, scholarly and democratic. The words that belong to "the people" are extremely powerful, especially when combined as idioms and turns of phrase. These colloquialisms can make a native language colorful and create mental images that either stand uniquely on their own or share similarities with another language. In essence, idioms are the most poetic version of popular knowledge that can almost become a dogma that everyone practices, but nobody really knows.

When I was young, idioms were an everyday thing: I used to listen to and repeat them, but I usually ignored their meanings and origins. Later, in high school, to alleviate the intensity of Latin class, I would have fun with classmates by translating Italian idioms into Latin. All of a sudden

This book was originally written in Italian as *Una Mela al Giorno* and published by Nomos in 2020. I wrote it to underscore the differences (and similarities) in expressing common concepts, especially when living abroad—as I was living in Seattle, Washington.

Writing about this gap between cultures is also a way to bring people together: showing how we may be different but we think alike, and just express ourselves with different words, pictures, shades, and colors.

"Don't look a gift horse in the mouth" was transformed into *"In equo donato non videtur in ore."* But it turns out that the Romans already made use of this same imagery in their established phrasing: *"Noli equi dentes inspicere donate"* (literally: "Never inspect the teeth of a given horse").

When I moved to the United States, the universe of idioms opened itself to me to a great degree: I developed an enthusiasm, and sometimes a need, for explaining a perfectly appropriate and specific image (to me, and other Italian speakers) within a given context. However, my attempt at translating the idiom into English often ended in a clumsy explanation that too often came across as completely senseless. Because each proverb finds its roots in the sociocultural and geopolitical contexts in which it was formed, that necessary context, fortunately or unfortunately—depending on your point of view—can be quite foreign to those who don't come from that same place.

Considering that "To translate is to betray, and often translating is like having dentures and not real teeth, or like wearing a wig or protheses of different types*," I am delighted to share this collection of idioms that ended up in a drawer for a decade. Its publication is also possible in

---

How to Write a Thesis by Umberto Eco

part thanks to Daniele's stunning illustrations and the collaboration with my friend Marianna. The result is a charming book that is ready to be devoured by anyone who is fascinated by language. Through it, you will discover that there are both similarities and differences across these common idioms that can either bring you closer to or further away from that which is "foreign."

Who Is "Foreign" Anyway?

Now more than ever, in the heterogeneous societies where we live, it's important to consider that "the stranger" can exist in all of us. From a relativist perspective, we are foreigners anytime we visit or move to another country, and differences in language can impose a barrier that is difficult to overcome. Keeping this in mind, this handbook compares idioms in four languages, serving as a useful tool for those who are eager to use the correct expression in the course of their travels—or are simply curious about other cultures.

It's raining cats and dogs

WHY DO WE SAY THAT?

In **English**, the imagery for this idiom invokes cats and dogs as protagonists that are "raining" from the sky. Evidently this originates from the phonetic similarity with the Greek expression *cata doxa*, which indicates an atypical and unexpected situation.

The diminutive of basin, *catinella*, is a small, shallow bowl often used for washing hands, faces, or clothes. The expression *a catinelle* indicates a large quantity, specifically of fluids. As such, the idiom in **Italian** implies a torrential rain caused by basins of water being dumped from the sky.

In **Spanish**, on the other hand, frogs (*sapos*) and snakes (*culebras*) are what fall from the sky, creating a wild nightmare that no one would wish for. This combination is also filled with magical realism and features in other Spanish sayings: for example, *echar sapos y culebras* ("throw frogs and snakes to the sky": to curse or swear at someone) and *tragar sapos y culebras* ("swallow frogs and snakes": to endure someone or something particularly unpleasant).

Finally, the **French** expression features strings, or ropes, instead, with the idea being that threads of water are coming down continuously and intensely.

It's raining
cats and dogs

Piove a catinelle

[It's raining basins]

Llover sapos y culebras

[It's raining frogs and snakes]

Il pleut des cordes

[It's raining ropes]

There's no smoke without fire

WHY DO WE SAY THAT?

The Roman author Plautus wrote in his 200 BCE play *Curculio*, also called *The Weevil*, "*Flamma fumo est proxima*" or "flame immediately follows smoke," which serves as a warning to keep an eye out for unexpected hazards before they begin.

In **English**, **Spanish**, and **French**, this same phrasing is shared across all three languages. It is a great reminder to be conscious and pay attention in our surroundings to avoid getting burned!

In **Italian**, a similar concept has a slightly different phrasing, with food involved: *Non c'è fumo senza arrosto* literally translates as "there is not smoke without roast." The pleasant-smelling smoke that arrives from a neighbor's backyard might suggest a barbecue is happening, like a sort of "warning sign."

There's
no smoke
without fire

No hay
humo
sin fuego

Il n'y a pas
de fumée
sans feu

Non c'è fumo senza arrosto

[There is not smoke without a roast]

Drowning in a glass of water

WHY DO WE SAY THAT?

To drown or sink in a glass of water is an expression used in situations in which we surrender even if the difficulties are minimal. The phrase is often preceded by "don't" as a command, encouraging a person not to lose faith or give up when facing easy obstacles. Once again, this idiom is univocal across the four languages, though the **Italian** verb also translates as "get lost" and the **French** offers an interesting lexical fun fact. The French verb *noyer* has the double meaning of drowning and wrecking, often used when a car engine has been flooded with too much gas. From that context, the "drowning" implies being stuck in situations where chaos takes over and it's difficult to be rational and clearheaded in how to behave. A related **English** phrase is to make a mountain out of a molehill.

| Drowning in a glass of water | Ahogarse en un vaso de agua | Se noyer dans un verre d'eau |

Perdersi in
un bicchiere d'acqua

[Get lost/sink in a glass of water]

A bird in the hand is worth two in the bush

WHY DO WE SAY THAT?

"Those who are satisfied enjoy" is at the core of this idiom. The phrase suggests that appreciating what one already has is better than wanting more and risking an uncertain situation in an attempt to gain it.

In **English** and **Spanish**, both expressions are linked to medieval falconry, and specifically how holding the predatory bird in your hand (the falcon) is a certainty in opposition to what might be hidden in the bushes or in the sky (*ciento volando*—one hundred flying birds), which could be of less value.

In **Italian**, the imagery used is of the egg that represents certainty in the present versus the chicken that symbolizes a future potentially richer but not guaranteed.

The **French** language employs a more direct idea: don't let your prey go (the verb *lâcher* means to loosen or slacken) for its shadow—in other words for nothing, or a projection of reality.

A bird in the hand is worth
two in the bush

Meglio un uovo oggi che una gallina domani

[Better an egg today than a chicken tomorrow]

Más vale pájaro en mano que ciento volando

[Better to have a bird in hand than a hundred flying]

Il ne faut pas lâcher
la proie pour l'ombre

[Don't give up the prey for the shadow]

An apple a day keeps the doctor away

WHY DO WE SAY THAT?

Originally from Central Asia, where it has been cultivated since the Neolithic period, the apple fruit arrived in the West thanks to the Romans. It has represented both immortality and sin, and it was the point of contention (Italians say *il pomo della discordia*, literally "the apple of discord") that caused the Trojan War.

Despite the well-known trouble the apple has caused, this idiom encourages eating one per day for its beneficial properties. It is one of the most famous proverbs across the languages, probably in part due to the phonetic nature of the words that create rhyming couplets (day-away: *giorno-torno; día-ahorraría; pomme-homme*) and make it especially easy to remember.

Since the phrase guarantees that eating a daily apple will keep you in good health, let's all embrace this most ancient elixir of youth and longevity!

An apple a
day keeps the
doctor away

Una mela al
giorno toglie
il medico di torno

Una manzana
cada día de médico
te ahorraría

Chaque jour
une pomme conserve
son homme

Don't count your chickens before they hatch

WHY DO WE SAY THAT?

In **English**, the saying nods to a popular folktale titled
"The Milkmaid and Her Pail," where the protagonist is
excited to sell her milk and starts pondering all the things
she could do and buy with the money. Among her wishes
is to acquire eggs that will one day hatch many chickens
to then be sold, and so on. However, she gets distracted
by her daydreaming and falls, spilling all the milk and
ending up with a broken pail and broken dreams.

The **Italian** expression comes from *Non dire quattro se
non ce l'hai nel sacco*, meaning not to be confident in
good fortune until you actually possess it. This phrase has
its origins in the rural farming world ("don't count four
until you have it") and later evolved into imagery of the
cat, agile and unpredictable—especially when trying to
escape—unless it is trapped in a sack.

In **Spanish**, the same sentiment is contained in a scenario that is reminiscent of Don Quixote: Don't ride the
horse before you saddle it.

The **French** adapted Aesop's fable "The Travelers and
the Bear" in the Middle Ages, which tells the story of
two young men who have plotted to sell the fur of a bear
before even killing the animal. In this case, just like the
poor milkmaid, all their dreams fall apart when the bear
frightens the hunters, leaving them empty-handed.

Don't count your chickens
before they hatch

Non dire gatto se non ce l'hai nel sacco

[Don't say cat if you don't have it in the sack]

No montes el caballo antes de ensillarlo

[*Don't ride the horse before saddling it*]

ll ne faut pas vendre
la peau de l'ours avant de l'avoir tué

[Don't sell the bear's skin before you've killed it]

You can't have your cake and eat it too

WHY DO WE SAY THAT?

You cannot have all things simultaneously: that is the core meaning of this idiom across all four languages, though it is expressed in very different ways that reflect the culture of the respective countries.

Straight from Her Majesty the Queen, the **English** language applies cake to this scenario. It's definitely one of the favorite treats that is served with the royal afternoon tea, but it is impossible to keep it wholly intact and eat it too.

The **Spanish** uses location to explain its meaning: you cannot be in two different places at the same time. Literally translated, you cannot both attend *misa* (Mass) and *repicar* (ring) the bells.

In classic **French** style, butter is featured as one of the most appreciated ingredients in the culture. The saying goes back to the nineteenth century and alludes to the farmers who wanted to both sell their handcrafted butter and keep it for themselves.

In the **Italian** version, wine and women are the protagonists. The saying seems to speak only to men: you cannot have a barrel full with wine and your wife drunk. Although the proverb has a sexist connotation, keep in mind that it has ancient peasant origins.

You can't have your cake
and eat it too

No puedes estar en misa y repicando

[You can't be at Mass and ring the bells]

Tu ne peux pas avoir le beurre et l'argent du beurre

[You can't have the butter and the money for (selling) the butter]

Non si può avere la botte piena e la moglie ubriaca

[You can't have a full barrel and a drunken wife]

Don't judge a book by its cover

WHY DO WE SAY THAT?

This expression invites one to beware of deceptive appearances. The **English** idiom has the simple pragmatism of Germanic language: you cannot judge the quality of a book's contents simply by looking at its cover.

The **Italian**, **French**, and **Spanish** translations, on the other hand, say that just because a person wears a monk's robe doesn't necessarily make him a religious man, pointing especially to his actions. This proverb dates back to the Middle Ages when *oratores*—those who prayed—had a very powerful role in society.

Contrary to the Parmenidean principle that asserts the unity of "Being," it is good remember that what is visible on the outside doesn't always correspond to the inside. This seems particularly relevant in our modern society, which is too often focused on public image.

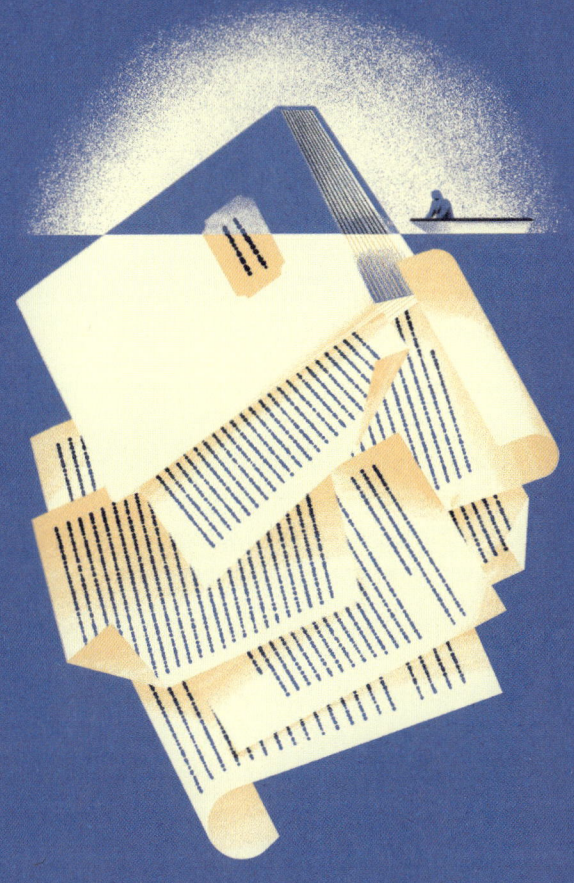

Don't judge a book
by its cover

L'abito non fa
il monaco

El hábito no hace
al monje

L'habit ne fait
pas le moine

[The habit doesn't make the monk]

Talk of an angel and you'll hear the fluttering of its wings

WHY DO WE SAY THAT?

Angels, devils, wolves, Roman emperors: when speaking of them, they all suddenly appear out of nowhere. Is it a coincidence? In the Germanic and Romance languages (specifically English and Italian), sacred figures are invoked, almost as if to discourage mentioning them by name—and potentially in vain.

The **English** calls upon angels, and in response the sound of their wings, while the **Italian** presents the same idea by way of Satan and his horns. Both imply that the person who mentions those supernatural characters might eventually be punished for disturbing them.

The **French** idiom has origins that go back to the traditional Latin expression *lupus in fabula* ("wolf in the story"), describing a situation where the person or the object that is being spoken of arrives at that precise instant.

The **Spanish** phrase sounds the most original. It adopts the image of a Roman king who comes through the door the very moment he is mentioned. Some linguists believe that *ruim* was originally used (in place of *rey*), to indicate the rude behavior of someone showing up unannounced and interfering in matters that didn't concern him.

Talk of an angel and
you'll hear the fluttering
of its wings

Parli del diavolo
e spuntano le corna

[Speak of the devil and the horns appear]

Quand on parle du loup on en voit la queue

[When we talk about the wolf, we see its tail]

Hablando del rey de Roma, por la puerta asoma

[Speak of the Roman king and he appears at the door]

As you sow, so shall you reap

WHY DO WE SAY THAT?

In **English**, this popular saying is a literal translation of the original Latin expression *Ut sementem feceris, ita metes,* and it is used to highlight the predictability of human actions. With the principle of cause and effect, it reminds us that good decisions and behavior can bring positive results and the same is true for negative repercussions.

The **Italian**, **Spanish**, and **French** also derive from Latin, by way of a phrase that instead calls upon the wind: *Quia ventum seminabunt, et turbinem metent.* This has roots in the rural world where disputes and arguments were common among farmers—it seems to be a warning in respecting a neighbor's land or risk receiving a "lesson" otherwise. A similar expression is found in the Old Testament (Hosea 8:7), in which the prophet Hosea rails against the leaders of Israel for causing violence and injustice and not following God's guidance.

No matter the source, the meaning is clear: beware of karma!

As you sow,
so shall you reap

Chi semina
vento raccoglie
tempesta

Quien siembra
vientos, recoge
tempestades

Qui sème
le vent récolte
la tempête

[He who sows the wind shall reap the whirlwind]

The pitcher will go to the well once too often

WHY DO WE SAY THAT?

When reading between the lines, the meaning of this phrase shines through: a streak of good luck will eventually end, or whoever misbehaves will be discovered sooner or later.

In **English**, **Spanish**, and **French**, the pitcher/*el cántaro/ la cruche* was the most used vessel for transporting water from a well or the closest natural spring before the time of indoor plumbing. Often made of ceramic, a pitcher could easily get broken during transit, since it was often placed on the head and a person could lose their balance if distracted. Hence the more often it is used, the more likely it is to break.

Italian, on the other hand, makes use of the domestic cat to convey this same idea. The beloved feline adores strolling around both in the house and outdoors, and often sneaks into kitchens searching for fatty (*lardo*) snacks to eat. This results in the expression "the cat goes so often to the lard that she leaves her paw there," which implies that the human upset by the stealing will chop off her paw. There are several variations in Italian. One is about the fly: *Tanto va la mosca al miele che ci lascia il capo* ("a fly goes to the honey so much that it leaves its head").

Another version—much closer to the other three languages—is *Tanto va la brocca al fonte finché alla fine non si rompe*, or "the pitcher goes to the fountain all the time until it finally breaks."

The pitcher
will go to
the well
once too often

Tanto va el
cántaro a la
fuente que al
final se rompe

Tant va
la cruche à l'eau
qu'à la fin elle
se casse

Tanto va la gatta al lardo
che ci lascia lo zampino

[The cat goes so often to the lard that she leaves her paw there]

Appetite comes with eating

WHY DO WE SAY THAT?

This saying, consistent across the four languages, suggests that the more one has, the more one desires. In other terms, often your interest grows when it is cultivated and experienced.

The expression is cited by the French author François Rabelais in his book series Gargantua and Pantagruel. In it he wrote "*L'appétit vient en mangeant . . . la soif s'en va en beuvant*," which means "the appetite comes with eating . . . thirst goes away with drinking."

However, the oldest reference dates back to the poem *The Metamorphoses* by Ovid, where the author explains the myth of Erysichthon of Thessaly. Erysichthon was punished by the goddess Demeter for cutting down her sacred trees with insatiable hunger and thirst.

Interestingly, the etymology of *appetite* comes straight from the Latin *appetere*, which translates as "aspire to or desire" and also "to fill up or charge." The term expresses the need to satisfy physical and intellectual desires.

In conclusion, there's nothing to do but sit down at the dinner table, even if you aren't hungry, because your appetite will soon show up. But please take your time, because as the Italians say "*A tavola non si invecchia*," or "You don't grow old around the table!"

Appetite comes
with eating

L'appetito vien
mangiando

Comiendo
entra la gana

L'appétit vient
en mangeant

To split hairs

WHY DO WE SAY THAT?

If you are one of those people who are extremely meticulous and somewhat fussy, often accused of being pedantic by others, this expression is for you.

The **English** presents an image of a person splitting a single hair, distinguishing the ends in an absolutely insignificant gesture, the result of which will hardly be noticed from the outside.

The **Italian** phrase is very old and describes a nonsensical search for hair in an egg, which is absurd and useless since eggs don't possess any hair. The Latin word *pilus* (*pelo* in Italian) also contains the meaning of something of little value or minor significance.

In **Spanish**, the cat is at the center of the action and searching for its hypothetical fifth paw—that is, a total waste of time.

The **French** seeks to find a tiny beast, reminiscent of the action of animals that are looking for lice or fleas. Here again the maneuver of nitpicking indicates the behavior of someone who is obsessed with minor details.

Though varied in form, all of these idioms encourage us to avoid quibbling over unimportant minutiae and instead focus on what really matters.

To split hairs

Cercare il pelo nell'uovo

[Look for the hair in the egg]

Buscarle la quinta pata al gato

[Find the fifth leg on a cat]

Chercher la petite bête

[Look for the tiny beast]

The grass is always greener on the other side

WHY DO WE SAY THAT?

This saying refers in particular to all those individuals who suffer from envy and are constantly unhappy about and dissatisfied with their situation. Because the phrase is univocal in all four languages, its origin is very likely the same.

One hypothesis is that in ancient times, cattle and especially goats had a tendency to eat grass on the neighbor's land, and even for some reason preferring it to their own. In our modern consumer society, where competition can be aggressive and comparison constant, the proverb feels especially relevant. The rivalry has become almost a stereotype when we think about stately neighborhoods full of perfect family houses, with shining facades and immaculate lawns. In this case, the grass represents order, cleanliness, beauty, industriousness, and therefore the image that must be maintained for the eye of the observer who passes by.

An interesting fact, though, is that according to the Italian encyclopedia *Treccani*, the saying comes from the British romantic-comedy *The Grass Is Greener*, directed by Stanley Donen in 1960 and starring Cary Grant and Deborah Kerr. If true, we are all using a universal idiom based on this fun film.

The grass is always greener on the other side

L'erba del vicino è sempre più verde

La hierba del vecino es siempre más verde

L'herbe est toujours plus verte ailleurs

Don't poke the bear

WHY DO WE SAY THAT?

Each of the languages makes use of animals to convey this common sentiment. The **English** refers to a bear that seems to be asleep but is in fact aware of his surroundings. His appearance is misleading because behind the superficial tranquility is the potential for an unforeseen ambush.

Similarly, in the **Italian** *Dictionary of Proverbs* by Carlo Lapucci, the quote "He who disturbs without reason dangerous, overbearing, or foolish individuals will suffer the consequences" is a direct nod to the Italian translation as "don't wake (or tease) a sleeping dog." This well-known colloquialism advises you to not disturb animals or irritable people that are currently calm.

The **Spanish** language replaces bears and dogs with the wasp's nest (*avispero*) that should never be touched, lest an angry swarm of hornets attack.

The **French** prefers once again to use the cat: don't wake one up that's asleep. His quick and startled reaction could be unpleasant, as he might scratch you all over with his claws.

Every instance offers a great reminder that certain situations are better left alone!

Don't poke the bear

Non svegliare il can che dorme

[Don't wake a sleeping dog]

No remuevas el avispero

[Don't stir up the wasp's nest]

Il ne faut pas réveiller
le chat qui dort

[Don't wake a sleeping cat]

If you lie down with dogs, you'll get up with fleas

WHY DO WE SAY THAT?

Many of us have probably used this expression and very likely heard it from parents, who have a tendency to comment on their child's poor choice in company that could lead to copying and adopting the behavior of others. It's true: as a youth, the desire to blend in, mimic, and sometimes even pretend to conform to a specific group are often ways to feel safer. The real issue is when a negative habit is the one that is replicated with the excuse that "everyone does it."

Most likely the **English** originates from the equivalent phrase in Latin: *Qui cum canibus concumbunt cum pulicibus surgent.* While no owner wants to believe that sleeping with their beloved pup will result in infestation, the meaning is understood.

The saying for the other three languages is credited to the Greek philosopher Plutarch. The literal translation of the controversial word *lame* describes spending time with an injured or disabled person and mimicking their condition. We include the idiom phrasing here as literally translated in the **Italian**, **Spanish**, and **French** for historical and cultural context, including the word *lame*. The long history of this idiom has not caught up with today's view, which acknowledges the word "lame" as derogatory and rooted in ableism.

Essentially, if you care about your well-being, be mindful of those you spend time with and always on guard.

If you lie down with dogs,
you'll get up with fleas

| Chi va con lo zoppo impara a zoppicare | El que va con el cojo, aprende a cojear | Qui fréquente le boiteux, apprend à boiter |

[He who walks with the lame learns to limp]*

*Editor's note: While unfortunately still in use idiomatically in this context, we acknowledge the ableist origins of the word "lame." We recognize such language can be harmful.

When the cat's away, the mice will play

WHY DO WE SAY THAT?

The core of this idiom is the relationship between hunter and prey, alpha and beta. Specifically, all four languages underline the stereotypical relationship between felines and rodents, often spoken of and depicted in fairy tales and cartoons through escalating conflict.

Scientific research, however, shows that this is merely an overblown collective assumption that doesn't have much to do with reality. It's unclear whether the cat is actually a skilled hunter of mice, or if in most cases the agile rodents manage to escape. Perhaps it is less common than we like to think.

Either way, the meaning is crystal clear: in the absence of authority, the reaction is a mix of euphoria and carefree activity that can lead to flaunting or outright breaking the rules.

When the cat's
away, the mice
will play

Quando
il gatto non c'è
i topi ballano

Cuando el gato
no está, los
ratones bailan

Quand le chat
n'est pas là, les
souris dansant

[When the cat's away, the mice will dance]

Kill two birds with one stone

WHY DO WE SAY THAT?

Similar to other proverbs—for example, "When one happens, many happen"—this phrase indicates a succession of events linked together and characterized by a positive outcome. Since it is also said that "Misfortunes never come alone," we can only hope the same rule applies to the joys and pleasures of life.

The **English** and **Spanish** expressions call upon the same animal (birds; *pájaros*) but they are killed by different strikes: a stone in English and a rifle shot (*tiro*) in Spanish, respectively.

The **French** translation features a stone that can be used several times to obtain multiple benefits ("two blows"). The expression was documented by the sixteenth-century philosopher Michel de Montaigne, but it was very likely used even before that.

In **Italian**, you can catch two pigeons with one fava bean, or achieve two things at the same time. This imagery probably finds its origins in the forests where hunters would utilize an unusual technique to pursue wild pigeons: dragging a long string with a large dry fava bean at the end. Once the bird swallowed it, it was unable to expel the bean, thus giving it the same function as a hook for fish.

| Kill two birds with one stone | Matar dos pájaros de un tiro | Faire d'une pierre deux coups |

Prendere due piccioni con una fava

[Catch two pigeons with one fava bean]

Bats in
the belfry

WHY DO WE SAY THAT?

The general purpose of this idiom is to acknowledge having bizarre and eccentric ideas that are often unrealistic and irrational.

The **English** references bats flying around in the bell tower, or belfry—the highest point of a building—to metaphorically make a correlation with disordered thoughts in the head (the highest part of the body).

In **Italian**, the image of crickets in the head works as well: the insects are jumping high and fast in a uniquely wild manner. In **Spanish**, it is instead birds (*pájaros*) that are in the head (*cabeza*), similar to the Italian.

Likewise, in **French**, the ceiling (*plafond*) is the highest point of the room, but in this case there are no birds, crickets, or bats, but spiders instead. Just as these insects are often disturbing and allude to the macabre, so too does strange thinking.

Bats in the belfry

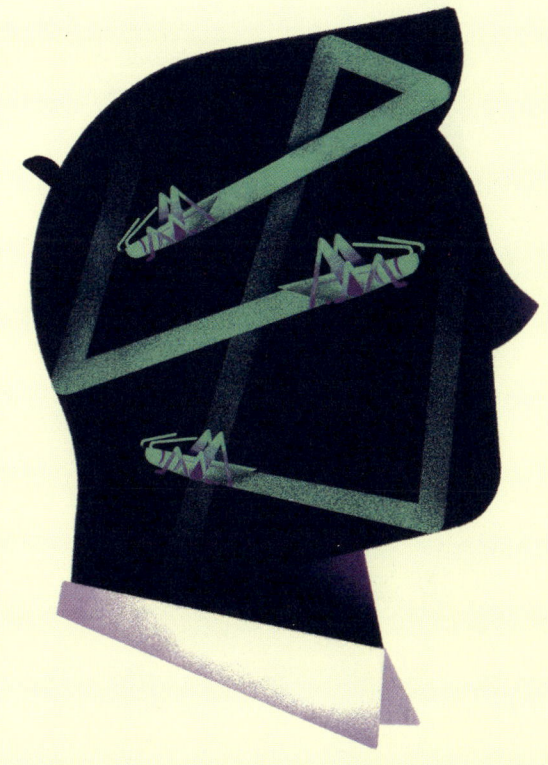

Avere grilli per la testa

[Have crickets in your head]

Tener pájaros en la cabeza

[Have birds in your head]

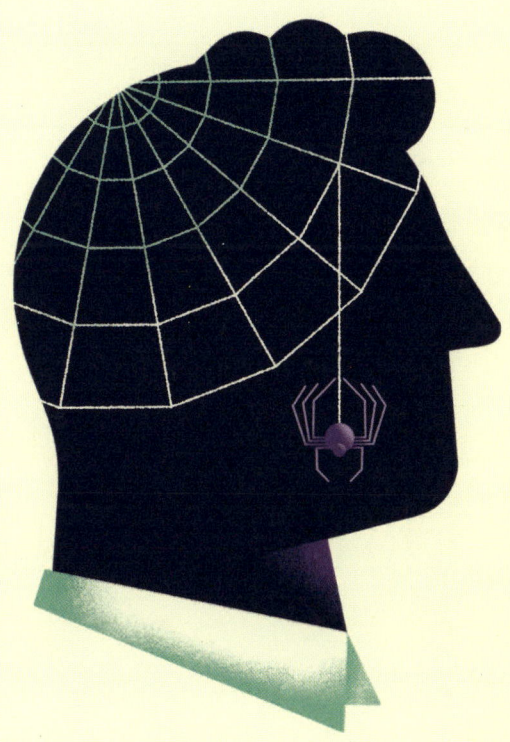

Avoir une araignée au plafond

[Have a spider on the ceiling]

Don't look a gift horse in the mouth

WHY DO WE SAY THAT?

This idiom instructs that we should always be grateful for the gifts we receive, even if they are of little economic value. It's also polite to show appreciation for the gesture of someone who offers us anything.

The saying is widespread and universal across all four languages, and it probably comes from farmers' jargon, when before purchasing livestock the countryfolk would routinely check an animal's teeth. Doing an inspection of a horse's mouth could reveal the age and health of the potential acquisition. On another hand, in a case where the horse would have been gifted, the examination was not needed and would be considered rude.

Another possible origin comes from the Latin quotation by Saint Jerome in the letter to the Ephesians, in which he writes "the gifted should inspect the horse's teeth" (*Equi dentes inspicere donate*), which was later changed to "don't look a given horse in the teeth" (*Noli equi dentes inspicere donate*).

In general, receiving a gift should always be a pleasure, and sometimes it offers an opportunity to overcome distrust and conflicts. When accepting any gift, be sure to show all your teeth with a big open smile!

**Don't look
a gift horse
in the mouth**

**A caval donato
non si guarda
in bocca**

A caballo
regalado no se le
mira el diente

À cheval donné,
on ne regarde
pas la bouche

Don't cast your pearls before swine

WHY DO WE SAY THAT?

In colloquial **English**, the proverb "don't cast your pearls before swine" comes directly from the New Testament (Matthew 7:6), and it means that valuable advice and other riches should not be wasted on those who are not able to appreciate them.

In the historical context, both dogs and pigs were considered impure, and consequently, neither deserved pearls, which were a symbol of wealth and grace. At the same time, those animals were compared to pagans who didn't deserve the sacredness of the Christian religion, considered refined and pure much like the pearl.

The **Italian** translation stems from the same religious source, and therefore the phrasing is identical.

French, on the other hand, substitutes the pearls with jam (*confiture*), whereas in **Spanish**, the proverb has a secular connotation with the giving of honey (*miel*) to a donkey (*asno*) instead. That expression is found in Miguel de Cervantes's masterpiece *Don Quixote*, where Sancho Panza uses it when replying to his wife, curious to learn more about the future of the two heroes/antiheroes.

Be it pearls, honey, or jam, the message remains the same: entrusting something of value to someone who doesn't deserve it ruins its preciousness, and above all is a waste of time.

Don't cast your pearls
before swine

Non si danno
le perle ai porci

On ne donne pas de la confiture aux cochons

[Don't give jam to pigs]

No se hizo la miel para la boca del asno

[Honey wasn't made for the donkey's mouth]

When in Rome, do as the Romans do

WHY DO WE SAY THAT?

Every place has its own unwritten rules, its own customs. This idiom suggests respecting and embracing other cultures' social behaviors and activities, even when we don't understand them. The **English** is quite literal with its mention of Rome and obviously comes from the Latin world. The other languages offer a slightly broader interpretation.

In **Italian** there are two related expressions that have the same meaning: "A country's customs are never shameful" (*L'usanza del paese non è mai vergogna*) and "He who doesn't respect traditions, has no manners" (*Chi non rispetta l'usanza non ha creanza*).

In addition, both **Spanish** and **French** express a concept of ethical relativism where no customs can be considered universal or absolute. This theory is well explained by one of its fathers, Michel de Montaigne, in his writing: "Every nation has many customs and usages that are not only unknown to other nations, but savage and miraculous in their sight."

It is critical to understand and respect the traditions of others, adapting to them when necessary, to promote a greater sense of coexistence.

When in Rome,
do as the Romans do

Paese che vai,
usanza che trovi

[Different countries, different customs]

Donde fueres,
haz lo que vieres

[Wherever you go, do what you see locals do]

Autre pays, autre coutume

[Other countries, other customs]

A leopard can't change its spots

WHY DO WE SAY THAT?

Nobody can alter their true nature: it is a certainty, although it can be difficult to accept at times. With a predestination perspective of this questionable proverb, an evil man can change his habits, his routine, his social life, and his environment, but he will always be bad.

English, **Spanish**, and **French** all source their translations of this expression from the Old Testament. The prophet Jeremiah asks the question: "Can an Ethiopian change his skin or a leopard its spots?"

Italian adopts either the wolf (*lupo*) or the fox (*volpe*) as the protagonist in its primary interpretation, but we can find similar expressions that highlight other animals. One is "the otter changes its fur but keeps eating fish" (*La lontra muta il pelo, ma continua a mangiar pesci*). The fox variation comes from the Latin expression *Vulpes pilum mutat, non mores*, used by the historian Suetonius to describe an episode in which the Roman emperor refused to free a guilty man who was asking to be forgiven, because he believed that he would never change.

It doesn't matter if it's a wolf, a fox, an otter, or a leopard under consideration, this phrase takes a strong stance on the infeasibility of changing one's nature.

A leopard
can't change
its spots

Un leopardo no
puede cambiar
sus manchas

Un léopard ne
peut pas changer
ses tâches

Il lupo perde il pelo ma non il vizio

[The wolf can lose its fur but not its vices]

Good things come in small packages

WHY DO WE SAY THAT?

Here is a proverb to emphasize the smallest among us! It concisely states that small things have the same—or even more—value than large ones. It applies not only to diminutive objects or items produced in small quantities, but also to people: a petite man or woman are equally worthy, and they can be even more impressive for their outsized personality and mental capacity.

In a broad sense, this saying spans across all four languages, but for the **English**, **Spanish**, and **French** in particular, it seems to suggest that we all need to appreciate the little gestures and joys that show up in our daily life.

In addition to the small barrel (*botte piccola*), we can find a couple similar expressions in **Italian**, such as "the best spices come in small sachets" (*Le spezie migliori stanno nei sacchetti piccoli*) and "small jar, rare ointment" (*Vaso piccolo, unguento raro*). There is also an antonym version: "the stronger the poison, the smaller the jar" (*Più forte è il veleno, più piccolo il barattolo*), meaning that wickedness, like kindness, can show up in small packages as well.

| Good things come in small packages | Las mejores cosas vienen en frascos pequeños | Les bonnes choses sont dans de petites boîtes |

Nella botte piccola c'è il vino buono

[In the small barrel there is good wine]

Putting the cart before the horse

WHY DO WE SAY THAT?

The meaning of "Putting the cart before the horse" is pretty straightforward: if you are in a hurry and reverse the logical order of things, the cause-and-effect relationship will get mixed up.

The expressions in **English**, **Italian**, and **French** are all equal in their countryside peasant origins, where it was common to haul farm goods by cart, lead either by a horse or oxen (*boeufs*).

However, the French expression goes back to the sixteenth century, where it had an erotic connotation. When the farmer was done working after a long day, he would enjoy the "peasant's rest"; in this context, the order of cart and horse made sense, because *les boeufs* (the oxen) alluded to the farmer's testicles and *la charrue* (the plow) indicated his penis.

There is a **Spanish** translation identical to the other three languages, but the phrase that is used most commonly in its place is "Starting the house through the roof" (*Empezar la casa por el tejado*). The idea of building a home from the roof down illustrates the lack of logical or sense in such an approach.

| Putting the cart before the horse | Mettere il carro davanti ai buoi | Mettre la charrue avant les bœufs |

Empezar la casa por el tejado

[Starting the house through the roof]

All that glitters is not gold

WHY DO WE SAY THAT?

All four languages agree in the sentiment of this proverb insisting that appearances are sometimes deceiving. Not everything that shines outwardly is actually precious. It is one of the most celebrated idioms, and is found all over literature, from Aesop to Chaucer to J.R.R. Tolkien and his *Lord of the Rings*.

In **English**, William Shakespeare's *The Merchant of Venice* uses the exact phrase in the second-act when the Prince of Morocco speaks to Portia.

In **Italian**, the phrase seems to come from the Latin proverb *Non est aurum quod radiat* ("It is not all gold that shines").

In **Spanish** the concept is expressed both by Miguel de Cervantes in *Don Quixote* and Fernando de Rojas in "La Celestina."

In **French** the saying seems to date back to the twelfth century, beginning with the theologian and poet Alain de Lille in *The Book of Parables*.

The long legacy of this proverb has allowed it to reach almost immortal status. Like a relay, the baton has passed through the hands of artists and writers who have used it time and again. We should all keep in mind its true wisdom and remember that not everything that looks amazing on the outside turns out to be so in reality.

**All that glitters
is not gold**

**Non è tutto oro
quel che luccica**

No es oro todo
lo que reluce

Tout ce qui brille
n'est point or

AUTHOR'S NOTE

Languages reflect our way of thinking and our collective sense of identity; that's why translation can often be challenging and sometimes inaccurate.

As an Italian living abroad in the United States for more than 19 years, I always thought I would really understand my new culture when I spoke and acknowledge deeply its language, expressions, idioms, and way of speaking. This is the motive behind translating *An Apple A Day* into English for the first time: I wanted to bridge the gap between my two homes. I also wanted to provide a window of insight into the four distinct cultures covered in this book, especially now when times are increasingly divided.

As a mother of children who were born in the United States, I promised myself to gift them the most precious present, speaking exclusively Italian for the first few years they were born, filling the sentences with expressions and proverbs, trying to imprint a culture of mine that I hoped would be theirs one day as well. In addition to my homeland's food, customs, and habits, they now possess my language. I couldn't be more proud.

This little book holds all the above and more.
I hope you enjoy it.

Grazie mille,

Michela Tartaglia
Author and Translator

ABOUT THE CONTRIBUTORS

Michela Tartaglia

Of southern blood but born and raised in Torino, Piedmont, Michela obtained a master's degree at the Alma Mater Studiorum University of Bologna. Her passion for food led her to open Pasta Casalinga, a lunch spot in Seattle's Pike Place Market where she cooks and oversees daily. This venture gives her the opportunity to share her sense of belonging to her motherland. She published a collection of her favorite pasta recipes from the restaurant in her cookbook *Pasta for All Seasons* in 2023 with Sasquatch Books. Michela loves to read, explore, and travel. She lives in Seattle with her two wonderful daughters, Viola Rosa and Eva Luna, and her Lagotto Romagnolo, Argo.

pastacasalingaseattle.com
michelatartaglia.com

Daniele Simonelli

A freelance illustrator from just outside Rome, Daniele has fought against autogenerated clip art for the past decade. Daniele briefly lived in London, where he kept nourishing his days by creating art. After his English experience, he returned to Italy with a great number of connections and international experiences. He loves illustrated books, jazz, and trekking. *www.danielesimonelli.com*

Marianna Rossi

As a designer and creative director, Marianna designs digital products and visual communication systems, often recognizable by an illustrative touch and a playful yet exacting approach to typographic choices and color combinations. She loves telling stories through design while connecting the dots between different languages and worlds that appear pretty far from each other. A passionate cinephile and music enthusiast, she also collects all sorts of printed materials she finds around. She lives and works in her tiny studio apartment in the historic center of Palestrina, an old, small town on the outskirts of Rome.
www.mariannarossi.com

Printed in China

SASQUATCH BOOKS with colophon is a registered
trademark of Blue Star Press, LLC

30 29 28 27 26   9 8 7 6 5 4 3 2 1

The authorized representative in the EU for product
safety and compliance is Authorised Rep Compliance
Ltd., Ground Floor, 71 Lower Baggot Street, Dublin
D02 P593, Ireland. www.arccompliance.com

Editor: Jill Saginario
Production editor: Peggy Gannon
Designers: Marianna Rossi and Anna Goldstein

ISBN: 978-1-63217-618-9

Sasquatch Books
1325 Fourth Avenue, Suite 1025
Seattle, WA 98101

SasquatchBooks.com